OR THE OLDER BEGINNER

THEORY BOOK

# ACCELERATED

# PIANO

## *Adventures*® *by Nancy and Randall Faber*

## CONTENTS

GUIDE NOTE BELLS

GUIDE NOTES

MEMORIZE THE LOCATION OF THESE "GUIDE NOTES" ON THE STAFF AND ON THE KEYBOARD

**1.** Name each **guide note** in the blank.
Then play, saying the note names aloud.

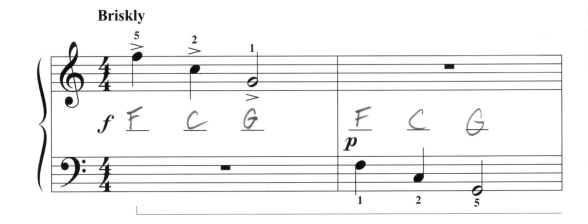

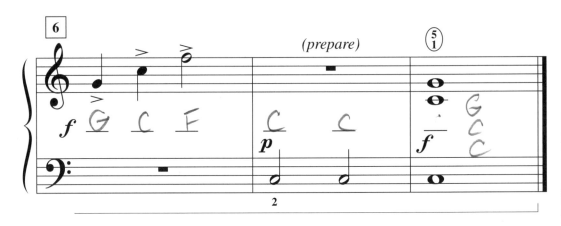

**2.** Create your own bell song using **guide notes**.
You may wish to use the hand placement at the beginning of the piece.

FF

**3.** Add **bar lines** to this 4/4 rhythm.

- Write the counts **1 2 3 4** under the correct beats.

**4.** Add **bar lines** to this 3/4 rhythm.

- Write the counts **1 2 3** under the correct beats.

**5.** Write 2 measures of your own 4/4 rhythm.

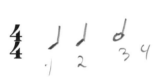 

- Write the counts **1 2 3 4** under the correct beats.

**6.** Clap each rhythm below with your teacher, counting aloud. Then, you clap **rhythm A** while your teacher claps **rhythm B**. Reverse parts and clap again!

a.

b.

# I and V7 Chords in C Position

**1.** Write two **half-note chords** per measure (**I** or **V7**) to add harmony to the melody. Let your ear guide you! Then play.

## Au Clair de la Lune

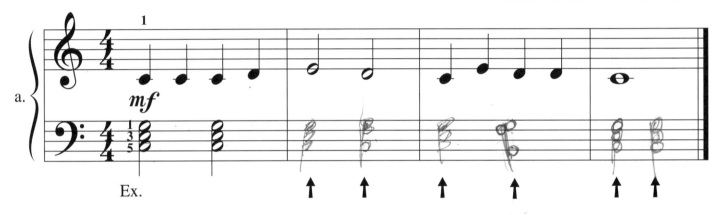

Ex.

- Write a **dotted-half note chord** (**I** or **V7**) in each measure. Then play.

## Little Stream

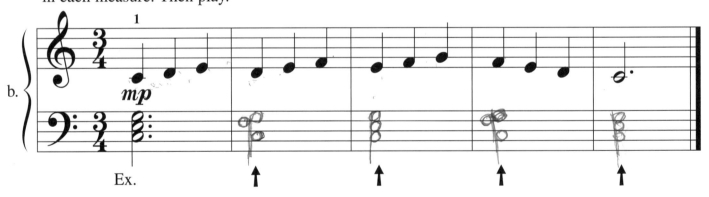

Ex.

**2.** Now compose your own **C pentascale** melody that sounds pleasing with the harmony given. Then play.

## Your Melody

Optional rhythm:

4

Sightread the musical examples below which use **I** and **V7** chords.

**Sightreading Hints:**
1. First, notice each **I** and **V7** chord in the music.
2. Set a steady beat by counting one "free measure."
3. Keep your eyes on the music (not on your hands).

**Bright march**

a.

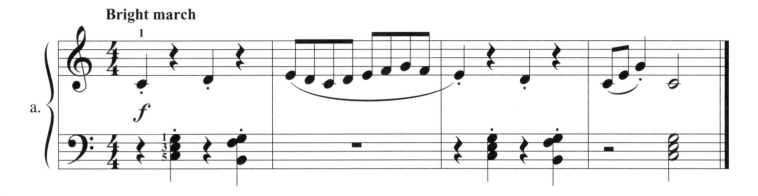

**Slowly waltz**

b.

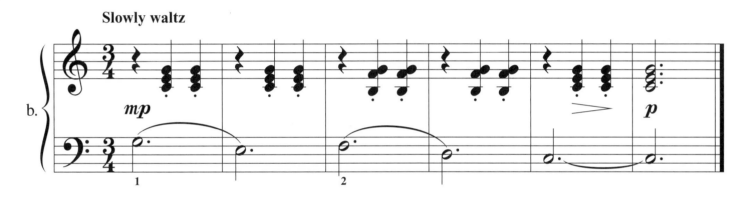

The **I** chord sounds *restful*. The **V7** chord sounds *restless*.
Listen to each example. Circle **I** or **V7** for the **last** chord you hear.

**1. I** or **V7**   **2. I** or **V7**   **3. I** or **V7**   **4. I** or **V7**

---

**For Teacher Use Only:**

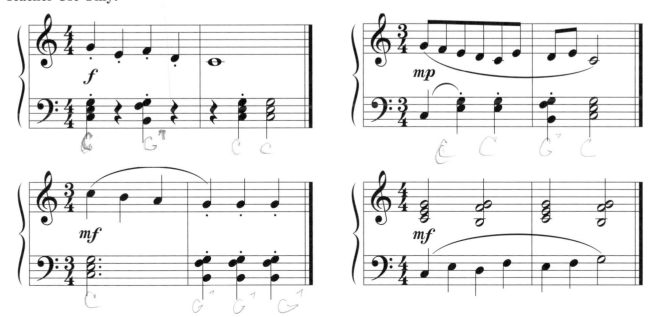

# I and V7 Chords in G Position

**1.** Analyze the **harmony** of each measure by writing **I** or **V7** in each blank. Then play the examples.

a.

b.

c.

Harmony: _____      _____      _____

d.

e.

f.

_____      _____      _____

**2.** Compose your own **G pentascale** melody that sounds pleasing with the harmony given. Then play.

COMPOSE

Optional rhythm:

The musical examples below use **8th notes** split between the hands.
Count one free measure of *"1 and 2 and"* before you begin.

a.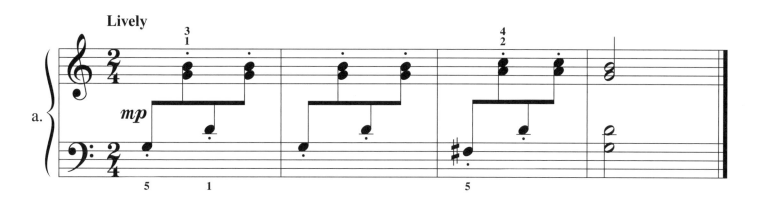

b.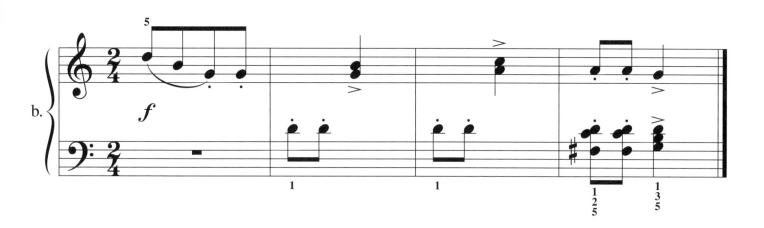

Place both hands in a **higher G pentascale**. Then close your eyes.
Your teacher will play a rhythm using **I** and **V⁷** chords.
Imitate the chords you hear.

**For Teacher Use Only:** The examples may be repeated several times and played in any order.
Continue, creating your own chord rhythms for the student to imitate.

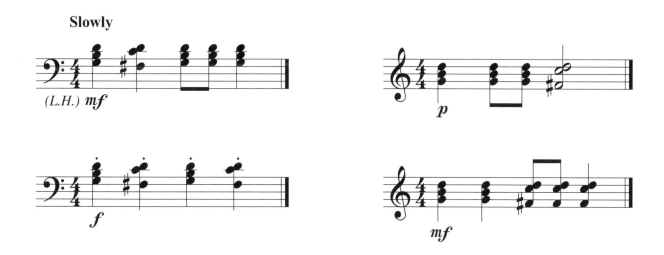

174

UNIT 2 — CFG DAE PENTASCALES

## Half Step Review:

From one key to the very next key is a **half step**.

**1.** Write **half steps** from Middle C up to Treble G. Use **sharps**. Play, using finger 2.

**2.** Write **half steps** from Middle C down to Bass F. Use **flats**. Play, using finger 2.

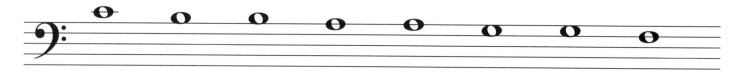

## New: Whole Steps

A **whole step** is made of 2 half steps.

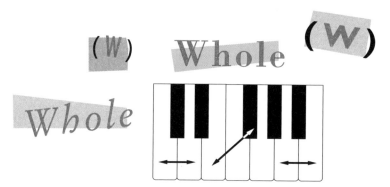

**3.** Draw a note a **whole step** UP or DOWN from each note below.
Use sharps or flats, as needed.

up a whole step

down a whole step

up a whole step

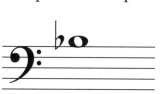

down a whole step

up a whole step

down a whole step

FF

For each example, circle **half steps**, **whole steps**, or **both**. Then, sightread each.

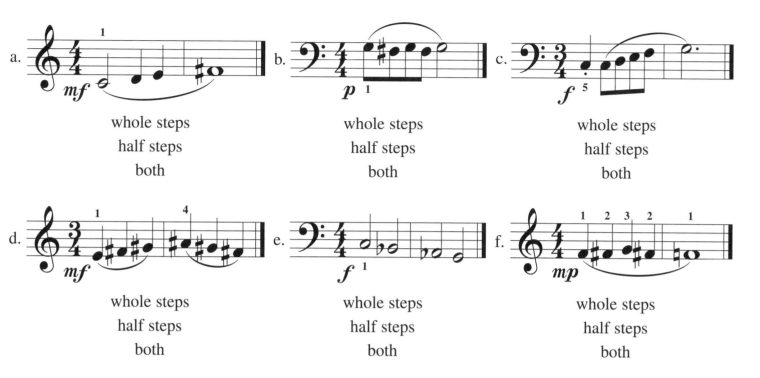

| whole steps | whole steps | whole steps |
| half steps | half steps | half steps |
| both | both | both |

| whole steps | whole steps | whole steps |
| half steps | half steps | half steps |
| both | both | both |

# Improvisation with Half and Whole Steps

To **improvise** is to create your own music "on the spot." While your teacher plays the duet, improvise your own melody following the directions given. Hint: The notes may be played separately or together.

- Play *any* **half step**. End on a repeating *high A*.

## Half Step Duet

**Teacher Part:** (Play 1 time before student enters.)

*Repeat over and over.*

- Now improvise with **whole steps**. Use this hand position.

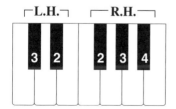

## Whole Step Duet

**Teacher Part:** (Play 1 time before student enters.)

*Repeat over and over.*

Lessons p. 10

74

9

# F Major Pentascale

**1.** Write the letter names on the keyboard for these pentascales.
Then mark the **whole steps** and **half steps**.
Mark **whole steps (W)** with a ⌐⌐. Mark **half steps (H)** with a V.

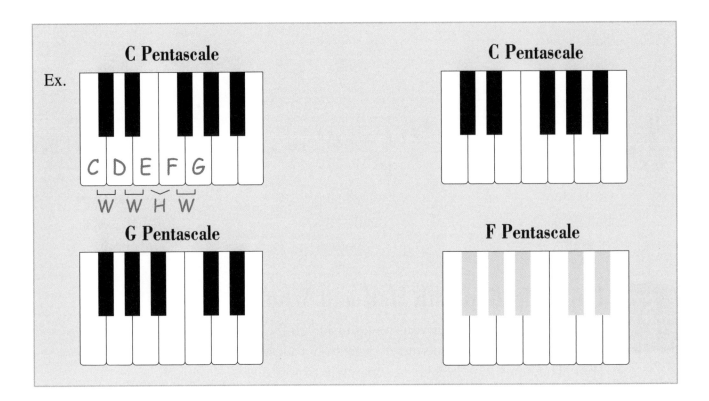

Ex. **C Pentascale**

C D E F G
W W H W

**G Pentascale**

**C Pentascale**

**F Pentascale**

**2.** Write whole notes on the staff to form each pentascale.
Mark whole steps **(W)** with a ⌐⌐. Mark half steps **(H)** with a V.

**C Pentascale**

W W H W

**G Pentascale**

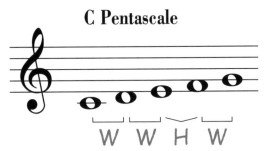

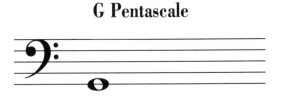

**F Pentascale**

**F Pentascale**

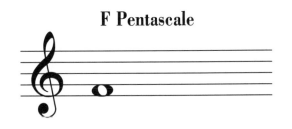

Remember the B-flat!

# Composing a Musical Question and Answer

A **musical question** is a phrase that ends on any note of the pentascale **except** the tonic.

The phrase sounds incomplete, like a question.

A **musical answer** is a phrase that ends on the tonic (first note of the scale).

It has a final, satisfying sound because it ends on the key note.

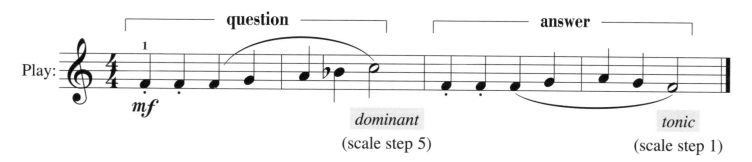

Play:

question        answer

*mf*

*dominant*
(scale step 5)

*tonic*
(scale step 1)

**1.** Compose a two-measure **question** and two-measure **answer** in the treble clef. Use notes of the **F Pentascale**. (An optional rhythm for your melody is given above the staff.)

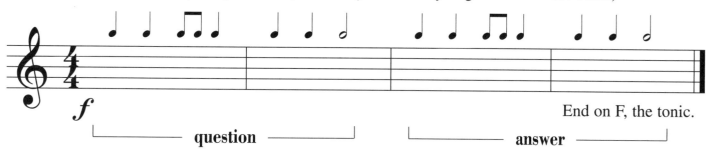

*f*

End on F, the tonic.

question        answer

**2.** Compose a two-measure **question** and two-measure **answer** in the bass clef. Use notes of the **F Pentascale**. Notice the time signature.

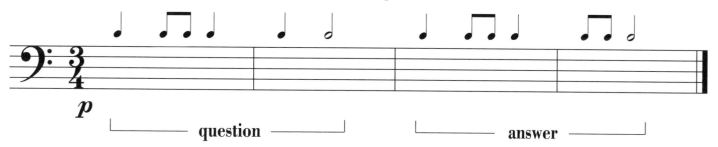

*p*

question        answer

**3.** Compose a two-measure **question** and **answer** using notes of the **F Pentascale**. You decide the treble or bass clef, the time signature, rhythm, and dynamics.

**4.** Transpose each question and answer above to **C** and **G pentascales**.

Lessons p. 13

# D, A, and E Major Pentascales

**1.** Write the letter names on the keyboard for these pentascales.
Mark **whole steps (W)** with a ⌴. Mark **half steps (H)** with a V.

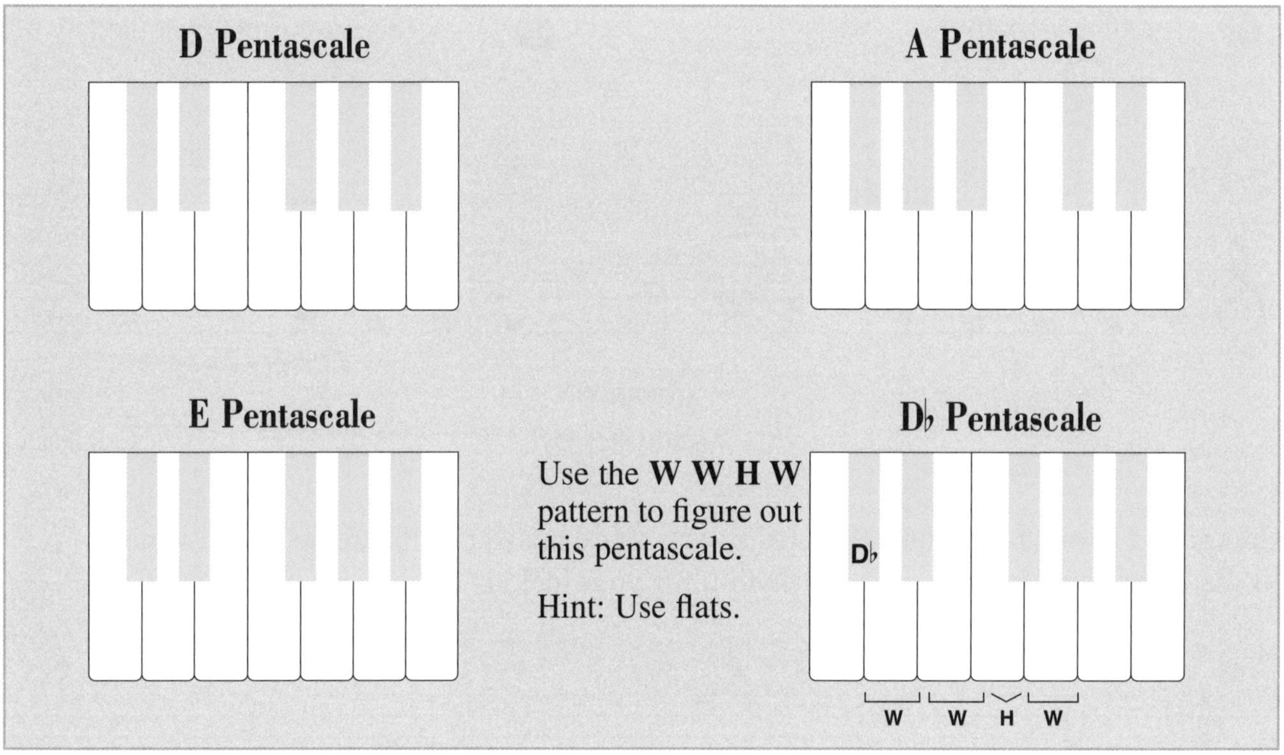
D Pentascale
A Pentascale
E Pentascale
D♭ Pentascale
Use the **W W H W** pattern to figure out this pentascale.
Hint: Use flats.
D♭
W W H W

**2.** Write whole notes on the staff to form each pentascale.
Mark **whole steps (W)** with a ⌴. Mark **half steps (H)** with a V.

**D Pentascale**

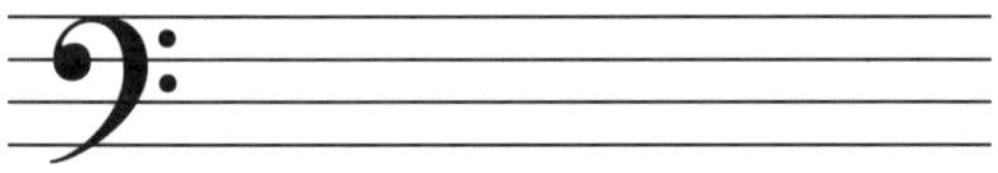

Remember the sharp!

**D Pentascale**

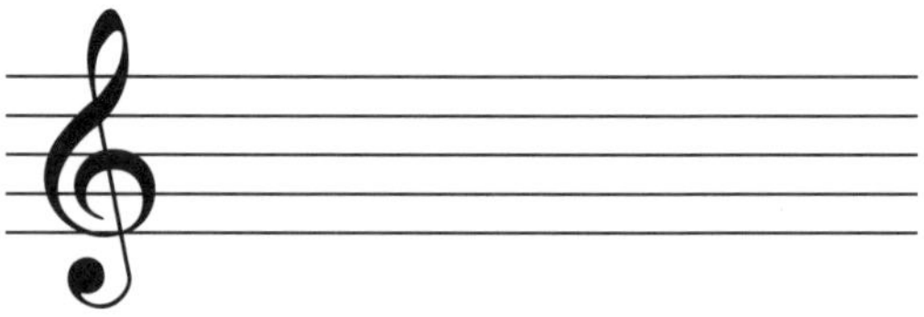

**A Pentascale**

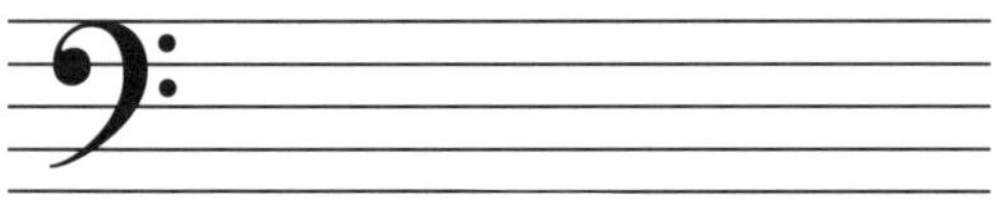

Remember the sharp!

**A Pentascale**

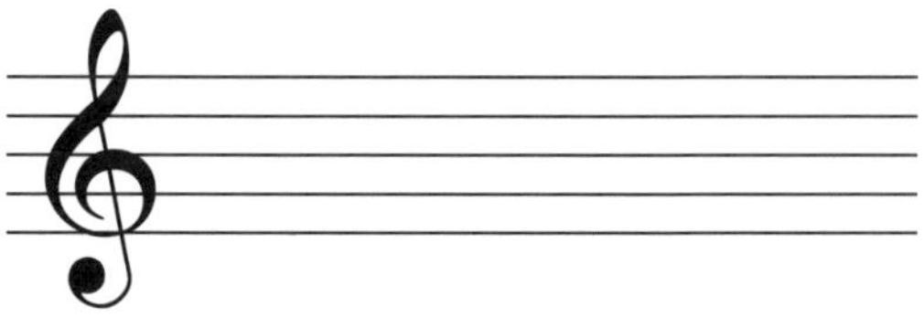

**E Pentascale**

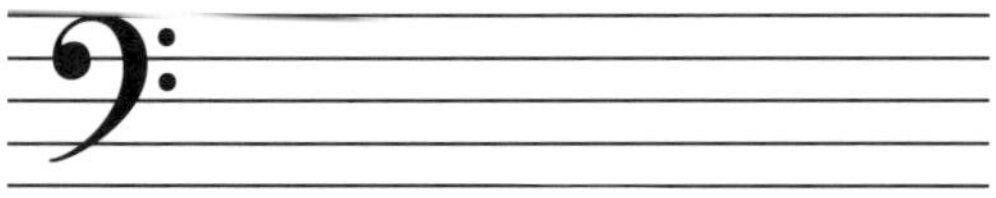

Remember the sharps!

**E Pentascale**

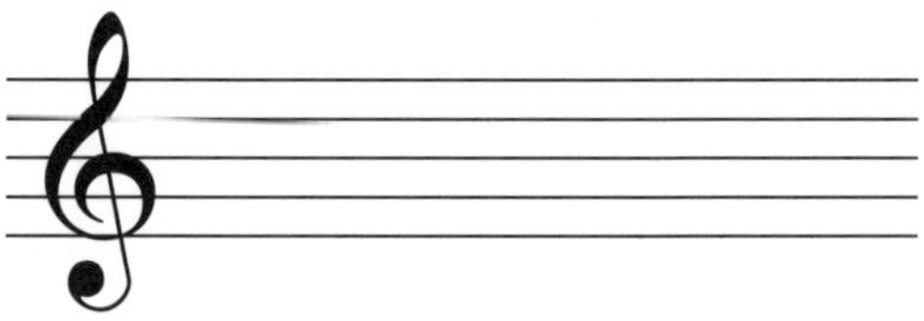

**Parallel Question and Answer:** The answer begins the *same* as the question.

**Contrasting Question and Answer:** The answer begins *differently* than the question.

- Before playing, look at the music and name the pentascale used.
- Circle **parallel** or **contrasting answer**. Then sightread at the piano.

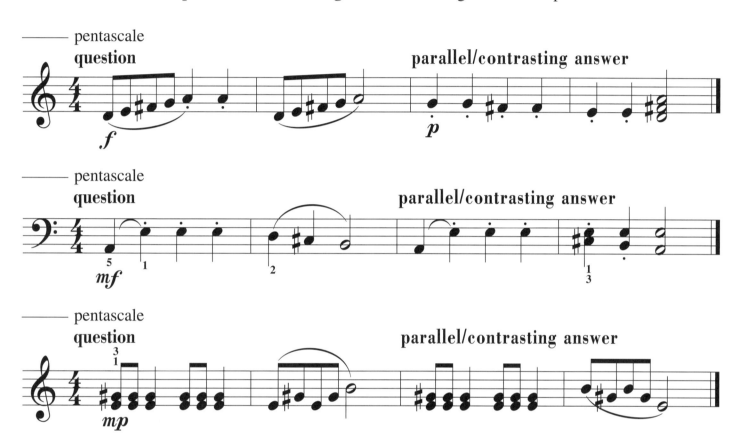

# Improvisation with D, A, E Pentascales

- Improvise your own pentascale melody with the teacher duet.
  You may enjoy experimenting with questions and answers.

**Student uses the D Pentascale**

**Student uses the E Pentascale**

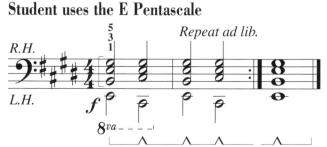

**Student uses the A Pentascale**

474

13

Lessons p. 15

# Inner Ledger Note E

A **ledger line** (short line) is used to show L.H. notes above Middle C.
Notice that inner ledger E is one ledger line *higher* than Middle C.

Ledger lines that are between the staves are called *inner* ledger lines.

- Play these notes for left and right hand, naming them aloud.

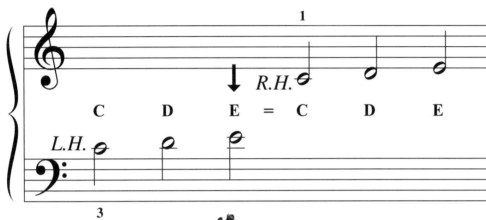

- Answer the Study Questions on the next page to become acquainted with one of Mendelssohn's famous melodies for violin and orchestra.

**Excerpt from *Concerto* in E Minor**

# Mendelssohn's Melody

(Study Piece)

Felix Mendelssohn
(1809 - 1847, Germany)

**Allegro appasionato (with passion)**

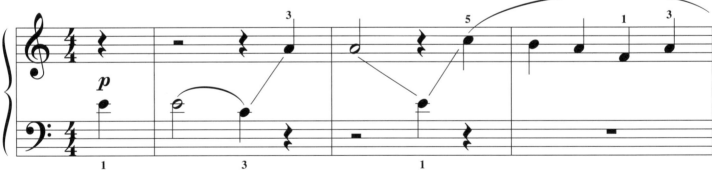

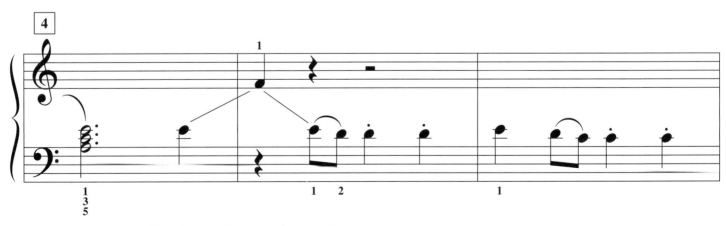

*concerto – a composition for solo instrument and orchestra.

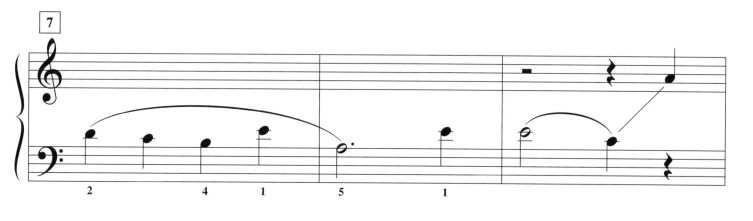

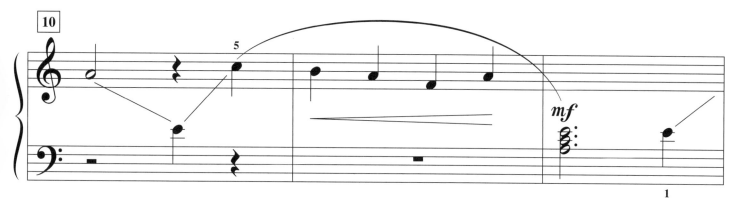

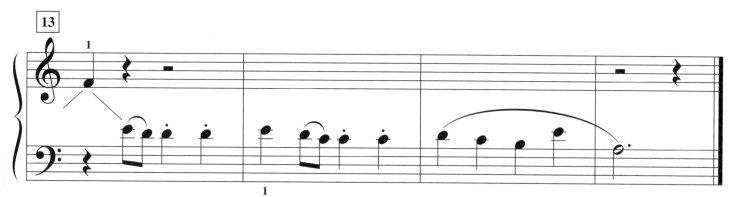

## A Closer Look at Mendelssohn's Melody

(Study Questions)

**1.** a. On which beat does this piece begin? _____ (*fill in*)

b. Put a ✔ above each note that is a **ledger line E**.

c. Put an ✗ above each measure with this rhythm:
(Hint: the rhythm may be split between the hands.)

d. Draw a **whole rest** in each empty R.H. measure.
(Hint: The whole rest hangs below line 4.)

**2.** Now play Mendelssohn's melody. If a digital keyboard is available, play using the solo violin or orchestra setting.

# Chord Scrambler

**1.** Unscramble these letters to form a **major chord** built up in **3rds**.
Then write the chord on the staff. Notice each clef sign!

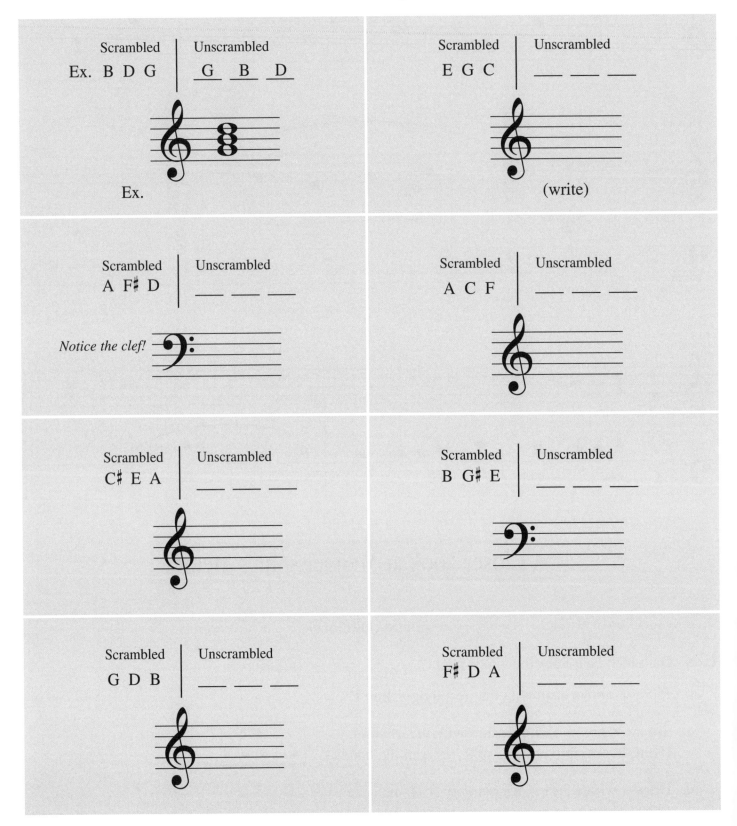

| Scrambled | Unscrambled |
|-----------|-------------|
| Ex. B D G | G  B  D |

Ex.

| Scrambled | Unscrambled |
|-----------|-------------|
| E G C | __ __ __ |

(write)

| Scrambled | Unscrambled |
|-----------|-------------|
| A F♯ D | __ __ __ |

*Notice the clef!*

| Scrambled | Unscrambled |
|-----------|-------------|
| A C F | __ __ __ |

| Scrambled | Unscrambled |
|-----------|-------------|
| C♯ E A | __ __ __ |

| Scrambled | Unscrambled |
|-----------|-------------|
| B G♯ E | __ __ __ |

| Scrambled | Unscrambled |
|-----------|-------------|
| G D B | __ __ __ |

| Scrambled | Unscrambled |
|-----------|-------------|
| F♯ D A | __ __ __ |

**2.** Make up a short rhythm on each chord you have written.

FI

These examples use major chords—*blocked* or *broken*.

- First, write the **chord letter name** inside each box. (Ex. D, C, etc.)
  Then sightread the music.

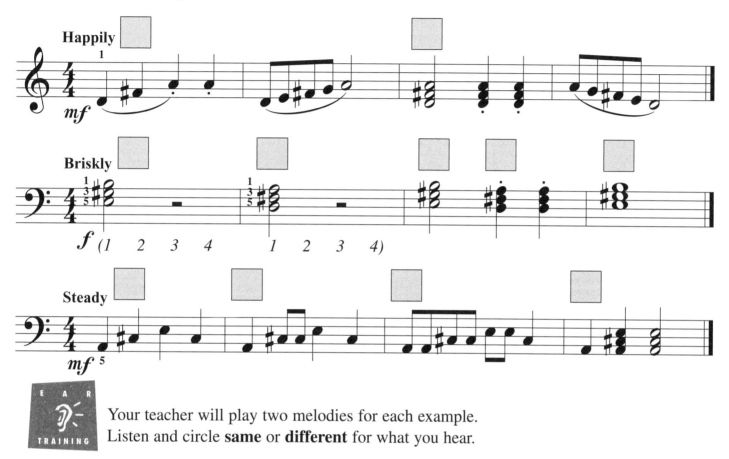

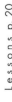

Your teacher will play two melodies for each example.
Listen and circle **same** or **different** for what you hear.

1. | **same** or **different**

2. | **same** or **different**

3. | **same** or **different**

4. | **same** or **different**

5. | **same** or **different**

6. | **same** or **different**

74

# Malagueña Variations
## (Exploring Major Chords)

- Name the **major chord** used in each variation of *Malagueña*.
- Then sightread each variation on the piano.

## Variation 1

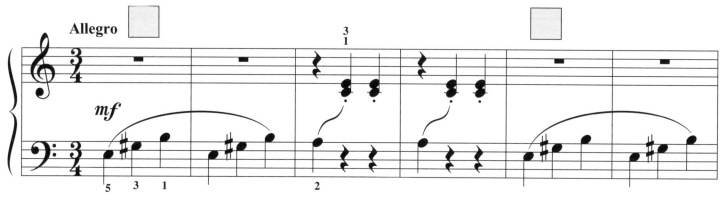

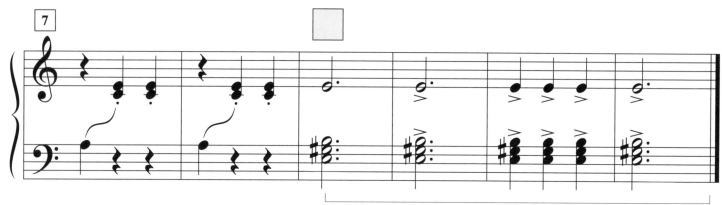

## Variation 2

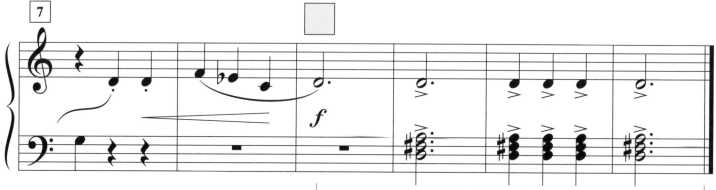

FF

# Variation 3

# Variation 4

# Minor Pentascales: Whole - Half - Whole - Whole

REVIEW: Major pentascales use the pattern "Whole - Whole - Half - Whole."

NEW: To form a **minor** pentascale, LOWER the 3rd note a half step.
The minor pentascale is **Whole - Half - Whole - Whole**.

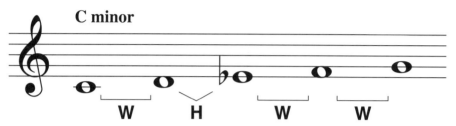

**1.** First, write the letter names to form **major** and **minor** pentascales below.
  • Mark whole steps with a ⌐⌐, and half steps with a V.
  • Then write the **minor** pentascales on the staff. Remember the flats!

Ex.

### C major pentascale

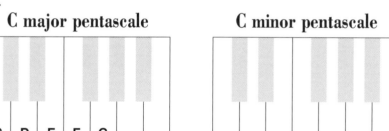

C D E F G

Ex: W W H W

### C minor pentascale

Draw:

### C minor pentascale

• Draw a 𝄞 or 𝄢 on the staff.
• Then write the minor pentascale.

### G major pentascale

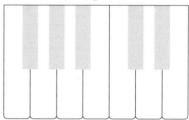

### G minor pentascale

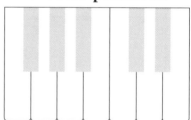

### G minor pentascale

• Draw a 𝄞 or 𝄢 on the staff.
• Then write the minor pentascale.

### F major pentascale

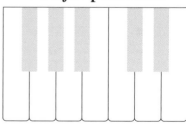

### F minor pentascale

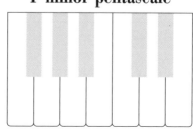

### F minor pentascale

• Draw a 𝄞 or 𝄢 on the staff.
• Then write the minor pentascale.

**2.** Play each pentascale you have written.

# Questions and Answers with Minor Pentascales

**1.** Name the minor pentascale used. Then compose a **parallel** or **contrasting** answer. (See p. 13)

—— pentascale

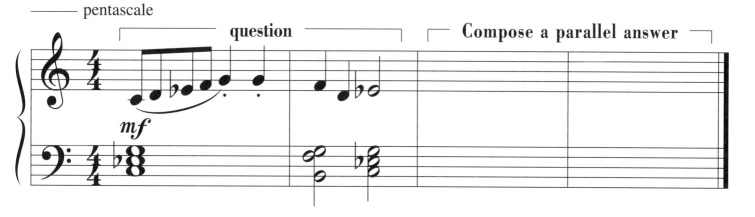

—— pentascale

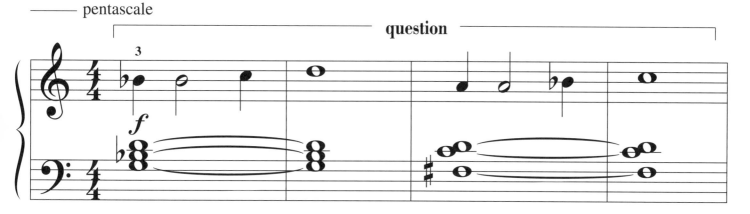

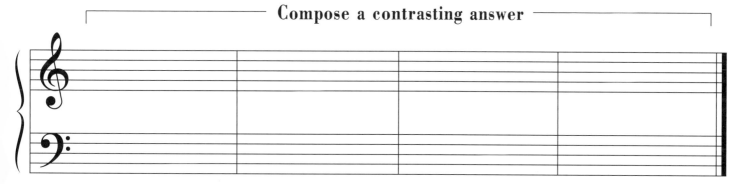

**2. Improvising with a Minor Pentascale**

c r e a t e   a   m o o d

* First, listen to the tempo and mood of the duet.
* Then improvise your own **G minor pentascale** melody with the teacher duet.
  You may enjoy experimenting with questions and answers in your improvisation.

**Teacher Duet:** (Student improvises *high* on the keyboard.)

474

Lessons p. 28

# Mysterious Rhythms at the Casbah

- Label the **major** and **minor** chords in the boxes.
- Write **1 + 2 + 3 + 4 +** to show the counting for the rhythm.
- Play these rhythms.

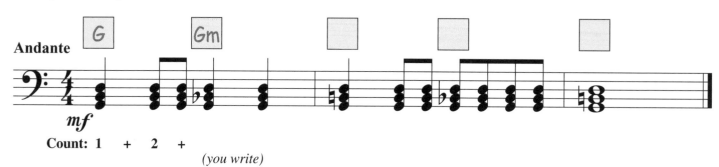

Count: 1   +   2   +

*(you write)*

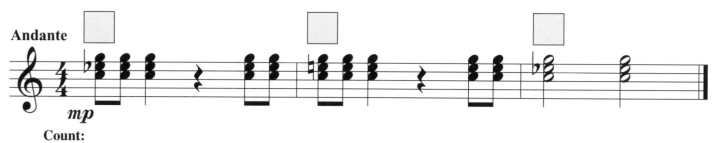

Count:

*(you write)*

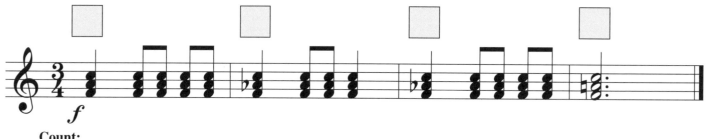

Count:

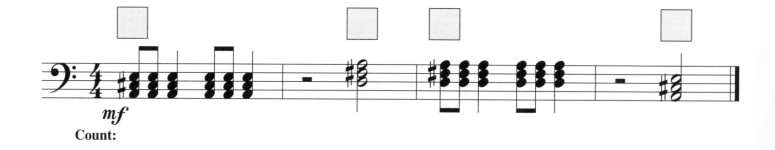

Count:

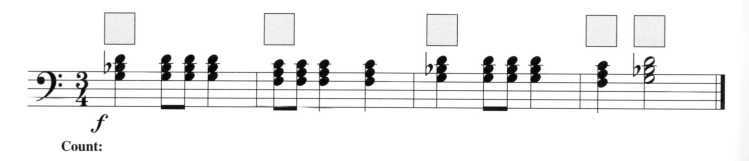

Count:

FF

# Review:

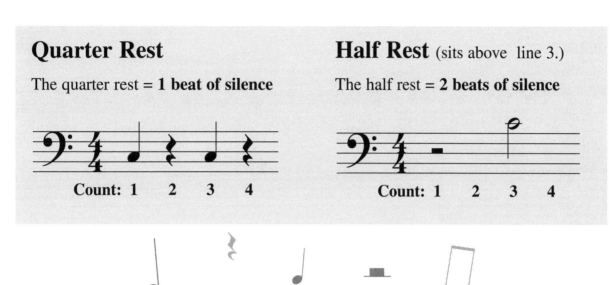

**Quarter Rest**

The quarter rest = **1 beat of silence**

Count: 1 2 3 4

**Half Rest** (sits above line 3.)

The half rest = **2 beats of silence**

Count: 1 2 3 4

# Your Own Casbah Rhythms

**1.** Write 4 measures of your own $\frac{4}{4}$ rhythm.

Use ♪♪♪♪ (4 beamed eighth notes) somewhere in your rhythm.

$\frac{4}{4}$

*(you write)*

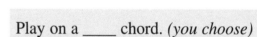
Play on a _____ chord. *(you choose)*

**2.** Write 4 measures of your own $\frac{3}{4}$ rhythm.
Use a ⸓ (quarter rest) somewhere in your rhythm.

$\frac{3}{4}$

*(you write)*

Play on a _____ chord. *(you choose)*

**3.** Write 4 measures of your own $\frac{4}{4}$ rhythm.
Use a ⸺ (half rest) somewhere in your rhythm.

$\frac{4}{4}$

Play on a _____ chord. *(you choose)*

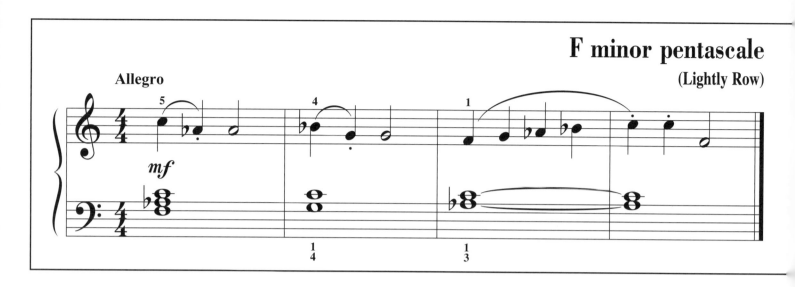

## Copyist on a Stormy Sea

1. Copy the 4 measures above on the grand staff below. Be sure to
   include everything in your manuscript: clef signs, time signature,
   slurs, staccatos, flats, ties, correct stemming, tempo mark, etc.

2. **Transpose** the 4 measures above to **G minor**.
   You may wish to play the music on the piano before writing.
   Include the same musical details in your manuscript.

### G minor pentascale

- Name the **minor** pentascale and sightread each example on the piano.
- Then write either *rit.* or *accel.* in the music where you think it appropriate.
- Play again with the *rit.* or *accel.*

_____ minor pentascale

# Bike Race

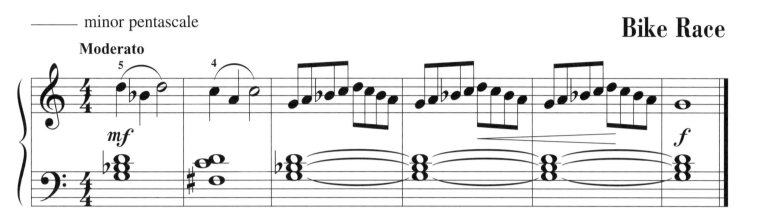

_____ minor pentascale

# Street Dancers

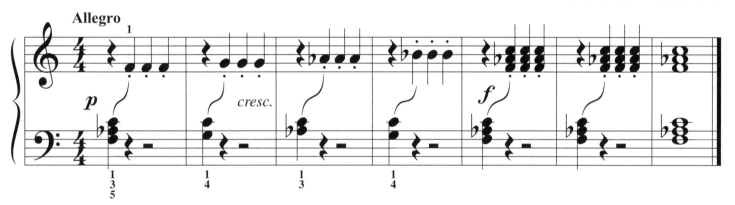

1. Your teacher will name a major or minor pentascale for you to find with your **right hand**.

2. Close your eyes. Your teacher will play a short example using the same pentascale, one octave lower.

3. Play back what you hear.

**For Teacher Use Only:** (The examples may be played in any order and repeated several times.)
Ask students to close their eyes as you play.

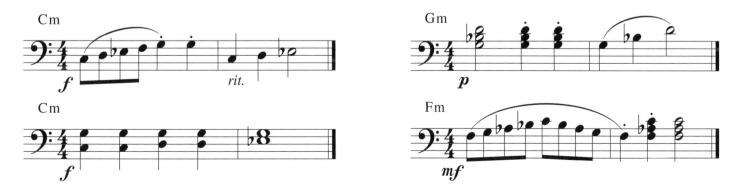

Note: It is recommended that the teacher continue this ear-training exercise at future lessons, creating more minor pentascale examples.

Lessons p. 32

# Major/Minor Sleuth at Work

| Major pentascale pattern | Minor pentascale pattern |
|:---:|:---:|
| **W - W - H - W** | **W - H - W - W** |

**1.** Name the major or minor pentascale used for each example.
Then circle the **major W-W-H-W** pattern or **minor W-H-W-W** pattern to match.

**Circle Dance**
Ferdinand Beyer
(1803-1863)

—— pentascale

**W-W-H-W**

or

**W-H-W-W**

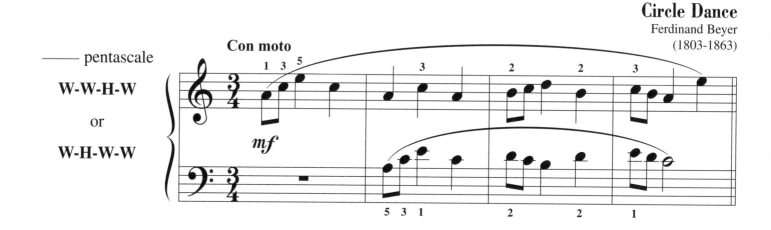

**Rondeau**
Jean-Joseph Mouret
(1682-1738)

—— pentascale

**W-W-H-W**

or

**W-H-W-W**

**Symphony No. 1 Theme**
(Excerpt from third movement)
Gustav Mahler
(1860-1911)

—— pentascale

**W-W-H-W**

or

**W-H-W-W**

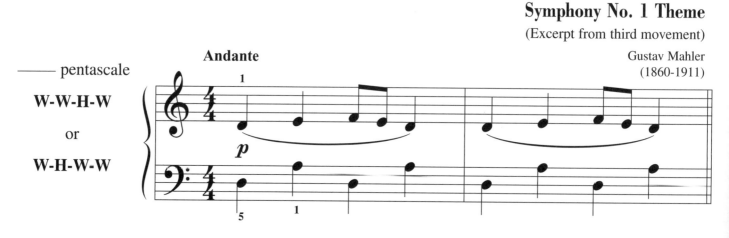

### Aria

(from the *Peasant Cantata*)

Johann Sebastian Bach
(1685-1750)

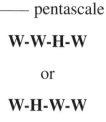

### Swan Lake Ballet Theme

Peter Ilyich Tchaikovsky
(1840-1893)

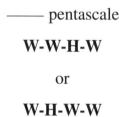

Excerpt from

### Violin Concerto

Ludwig van Beethoven
(1770-1827)

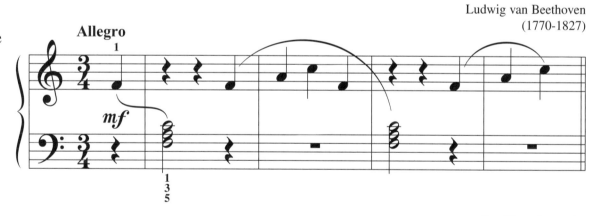

### La Tambourin

Francois-Joseph Gossec
(1734-1829)

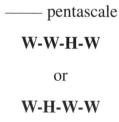

**2.** Play each example on the piano.

Lessons p. 34

## Lead Sheet in A Minor

**Chord References**: Practice the chords used in *Hey, Ho, Nobody Home*.

Am      G      F      E

In popular music, the "lead" refers to the melody.

A *lead sheet* is the melody *only*, with **chord symbols** written above the staff.

**1.** • First, play the melody only.

     • Then add L.H. **blocked chords** on *beat 1 of each measure* as indicated by the chord symbols.

# Hey, Ho, Nobody Home

**Briskly**                                       Traditional

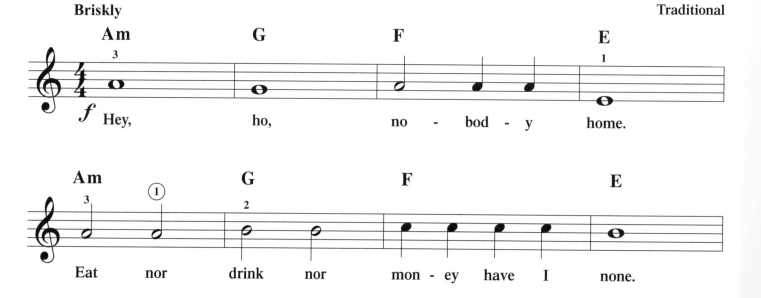

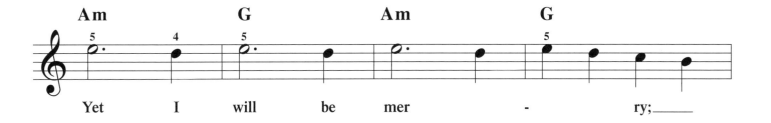

Yet    I    will    be    mer  -    ry;____

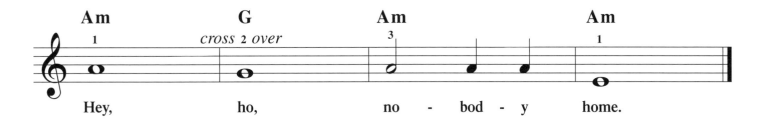

Hey,    ho,    no - bod - y    home.

## 2. Two-Hand Accompaniment: Broken Chord

When you can comfortably play *Hey, Ho, Nobody Home* using **blocked chords**, play a duet with your teacher, as follows:

- Your teacher will play the "**lead**" (melody) high on the keyboard.
  (Teacher Note: You may enjoy playing in octaves.)

- You play the **harmony** using the accompaniment pattern shown below.
  The left hand plays the *root* of the chord on beat 1.
  The right hand plays a *broken chord* on beats 2, 3, and 4.

**Practice Hint:** Practice this two-hand accompaniment s-l-o-w-l-y for a
                          steady beat before your teacher joins you playing the melody.

## Hey, Ho Accompaniment

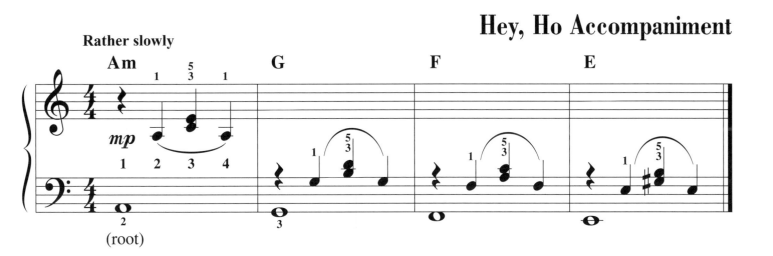

# Music Dictionary Match-up

- Connect each term on the left to the correct definition or example on the right.
- Can you play an example of each on the piano for your teacher?

|  | |
|---|---|
| tonic | |
| half step | |
| allegro | |
| a tempo | |
| W W H W | |
| dominant | |
| *accelerando* | |
| andante | |
| ledger note E | |
| $\frac{2}{4}$ | |
| whole step | |
| Cm, Gm, Fm chords | |
| transpose | |
| Dm, Em, Am chords | |
| W H W W | |
| E minor pentascale | |

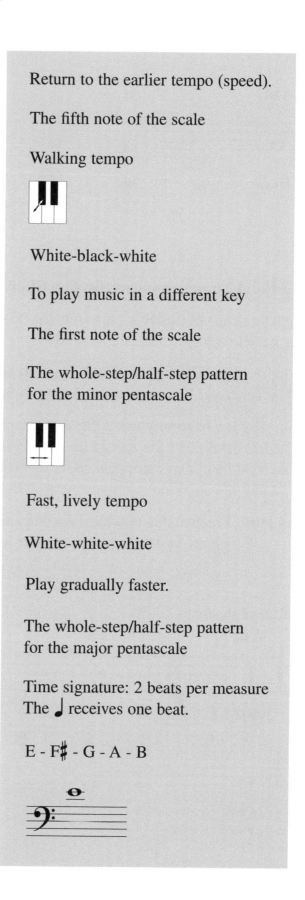

Return to the earlier tempo (speed).

The fifth note of the scale

Walking tempo

White-black-white

To play music in a different key

The first note of the scale

The whole-step/half-step pattern for the minor pentascale

Fast, lively tempo

White-white-white

Play gradually faster.

The whole-step/half-step pattern for the major pentascale

Time signature: 2 beats per measure The ♩ receives one beat.

E - F♯ - G - A - B

• Name the **minor** pentascale. Then sightread each R.H. melody (with repeats).
• Play the blocked chords with L.H. only, as indicated by the chord symbols.
• Then play hands together.

A **major** chord has a brighter, cheerful sound.
A **minor** chord has a darker, sometimes mysterious or sad sound.

1. Close your eyes as your teacher plays a short example using a
   major or minor chord.

2. Listen and say "major" or "minor" for what you hear.

**For Teacher Use Only:** (The teacher may play the examples in any order and repeat as often as necessary.)

Note: It is recommended that the teacher continue this ear-training exercise at future lessons,
      using other examples of major and minor chords.

Lessons p. 38

# Five C's on the Grand Staff

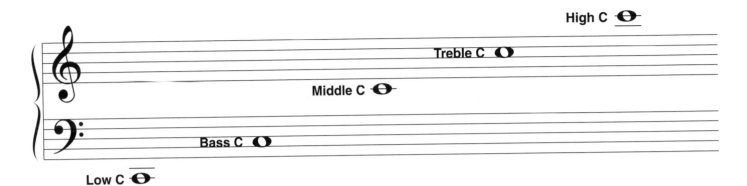

- Fill each measure with your own $\frac{4}{4}$ rhythm.

- Play your "Chimes on C" melody with the damper pedal depressed throughout.

# Chimes on C

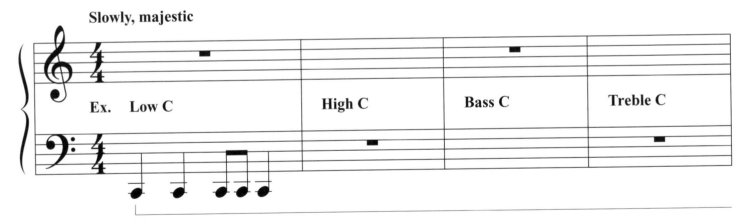

FF

- Name each R.H. interval in the box (2nd, 3rd, 4th, 5th).
- Then draw a *fermata* above each **L.H. half note**.
- Sightread at the piano.

Sing the opening of each of these songs on "la" with your teacher.

A **2nd** sounds like the opening to *Alouette*.

A **3rd** sounds like the opening of *For He's a Jolly Good Fellow*.

A **4th** sounds like the opening of *Here Comes the Bride*.

A **5th** sounds like the opening of *Twinkle, Twinkle, Little Star*.

Your teacher will play a **2nd, 3rd, 4th, or 5th.** Listen carefully and name the interval you hear.
(You may wish to hum the interval first.)

Lessons p. 43

## UNIT 7 · ARPEGGIO

REVIEW:

A **sharp** can be written on any line or in any space of the staff.

A **flat** can be written on any line or in any space of the staff.

**1.** Trace these sharps.

Trace these flats.

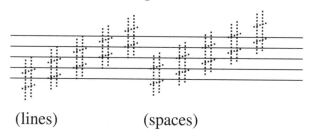

(lines)          (spaces)

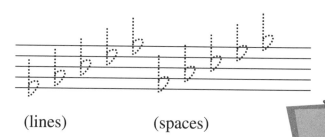

(lines)          (spaces)

**2.** Write **sharps** or **flats** to complete these **major** and **minor** cross-hand arpeggios and chords. You may wish to first play each on the piano.

# Cross-Hand Arpeggios

**C minor – write flats or sharps?** *(circle)*

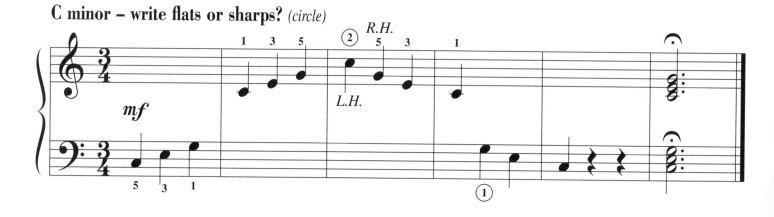

**D major – write flats or sharps?**

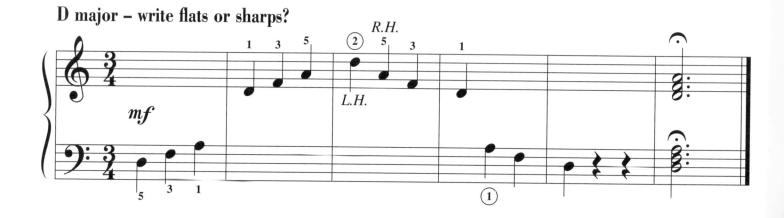

**E major – write flats or sharps?**

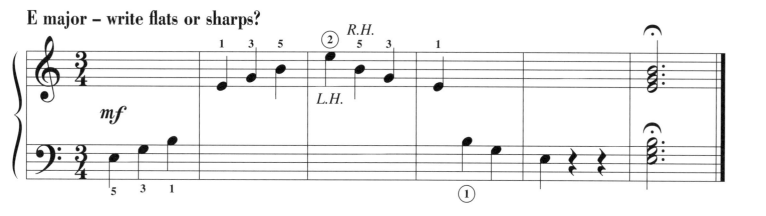

**F minor – write flats or sharps?**

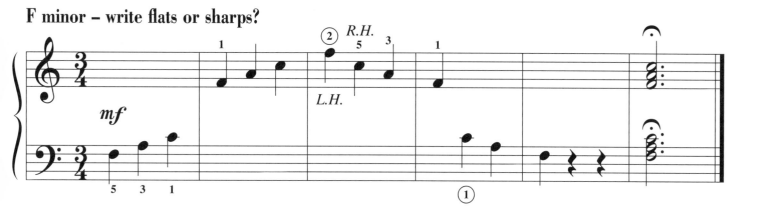

**A major – write flats or sharps?**

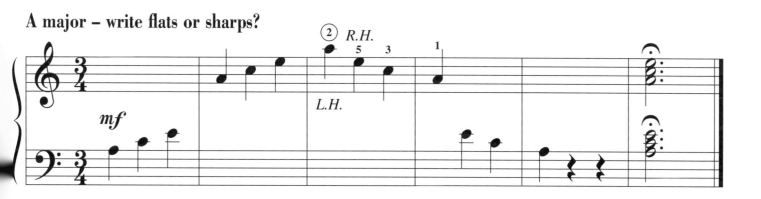

**G minor – write flats or sharps?**

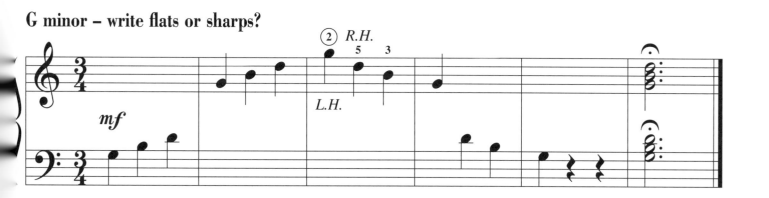

## Musical Form

The overall structure of a piece is called *musical form.*

This piece has three sections: an **A section**, **B section**, and the return of the **A section**. It is in **ABA form**.

A **fandango** is a spirited Spanish dance in $\frac{3}{4}$ time.

# Fandango

## A Closer Look at Fandango

(Study Questions)

1. a. Label the **A section**, **B section**, and the return of the **A section** in this piece.

   b. Write the chord letter name in the boxes for *measures 1-16*.

   c. Write a **parallel** or **contrasting** answer for *measures 17-24*.

2. Now play *Fandango* on the piano.

# Sixth (6th)

- On the staff, a **6th** is from:
  a line to a space or a space to a line.

- A **6th** is related to a **3rd**. Turning the notes of a 6th upside down (inverting) forms a 3rd.

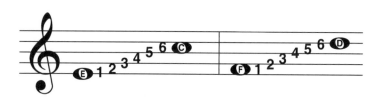

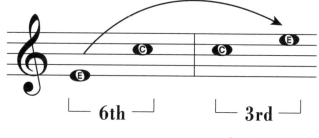

**1.** First, complete writing **3rds** and **6ths** for *measures 5-8*.

- Then name the **lower** and **upper** note for each interval.

# Chimes and Bells

(Combining 6ths and 3rds)

**2.** Play this piece on the piano. Listen to the sweet sound of **3rds** and **6ths**.

FF

- Identify each interval below (2nd, 3rd, 4th, 5th, or 6th).

- Then sightread the examples. Remember to set a slow, steady beat before you begin.

Intervals: Ex. 4th ___ ___ ___ ___ ___ ___ ___

___ ___ ___ ___ ___ ___

___ ___ ___ ___ ___ ___ ___

Your teacher will play the note given followed by a note a **5th** or **6th** higher. First, circle the interval name. Then write the second note you hear.

**Listening Hint:** A 5th sounds like the beginning of *Twinkle, Twinkle Little Star.*
A 6th sounds like the beginning of *My Bonnie Lies Over the Ocean.*

**Teacher Note:** The teacher chooses to play either a 5th or 6th higher from the given note. The examples may be played several times.

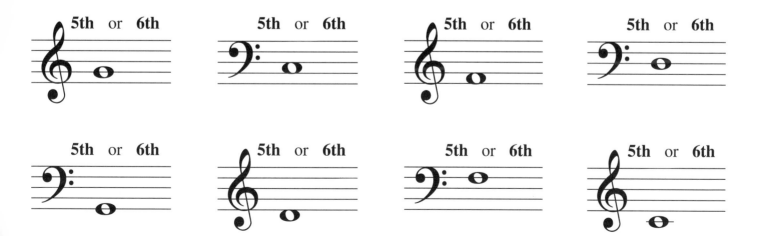

Lessons p. 50

# The C Major Scale

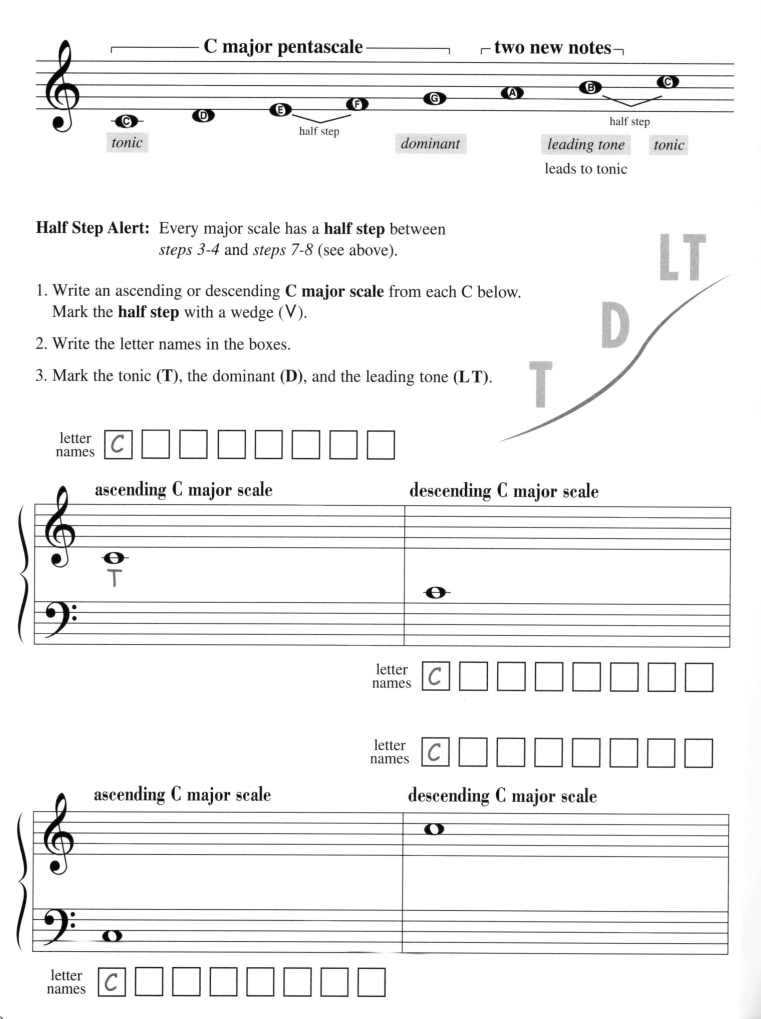

FF

Pretend you are a piano teacher helping a student learn a piece with the C scale.

- In each blank, write the correct fingering for the **C scale**.

- Then play the piece on the piano, carefully observing the fingering you have written.

# Jazzy C Scale Study

Hint: This is the scale in **contrary motion**.

Lessons p. 53

# C Scale Questions and Answers

**1.** Notice the ascending and descending C major scale are used in these musical questions.

- Does the question end on the **tonic**, **dominant**, or **leading tone**?

- Compose **musical answers** to complete the themes.

Q and A

## R.H. Theme

Compose a parallel answer.

## L.H. Theme

Compose a contrasting answer.

## Budding Composer

**2.** Compose your own theme with a question and answer that uses the **C major scale**.
Composer decisions: treble or bass clef? 4/4 or 3/4? parallel or contrasting answers?

FF

**Finger Substitution** means switching to a different finger on the same key. This sets the hand in a new position.

- First, look through each sightreading example noting the **finger substitutions**.
- Sightread the melody.
- Play again with **blocked I** and **V7** chords in the key of C major.

## Climbing

## Little Dance

Your teacher will play a short melody that ends on the **I** or **V7** chord.
Tell your teacher the chord you hear at the end.
Hint: The I chord sounds finished or complete.

---

**For Teacher Use Only:** The examples may be played in any order and repeated several times.

- The teacher may continue with additional examples of his/her own.

Lessons p. 56

# Key of C Major: I, IV, and V7 Chords

Remember the **I chord** is built up in thirds from **scale step 1**.
**NEW:** The **IV** chord is built up in thirds from **scale step 4**.
**NEW:** The **V7** chord is built up in thirds from **scale step 5**.

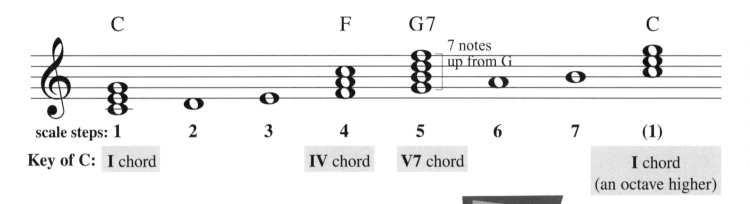

| scale steps: | 1 | 2 | 3 | 4 | 5 | 6 | 7 | (1) |

**Key of C:** I chord      IV chord   V7 chord      I chord (an octave higher)

**1.** Circle the *root* (lowest note) of each R.H. chord.

- Then write the **chord letter name** in the box above.

- Write the **Roman numeral** below the bass staff.

**Primary Rock**

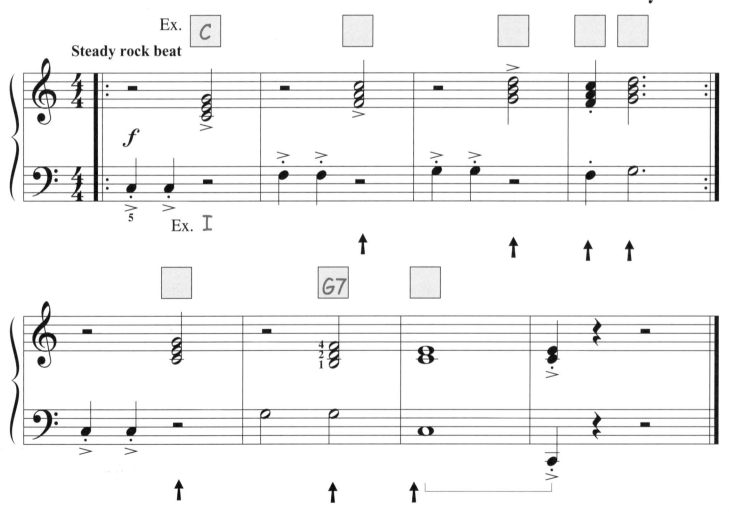

**2.** Play *Primary Rock* on the piano.

FF

# Chord Match-up

1. Write the **Roman numerals** in the boxes below each musical example.
   - Then draw a connecting line to the matching **chord letter names** to the left.

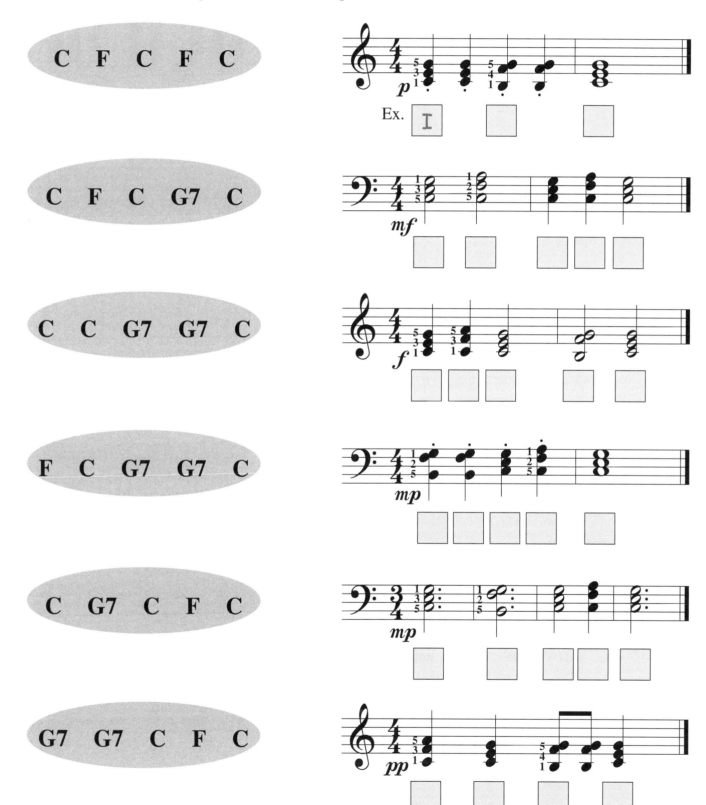

2. **At the keyboard:**

   - With your L.H., play all the chords in the boxes on the left. You are reading **chord symbols**.

   - Now *sightread* the chords on the right using the correct hand. (Check the clef sign!)

Lessons p. 60

# Lead Sheet in C Major

- Explore harmonizing this famous melody with **I**, **IV**, and **V7 chords** in the key of C major.

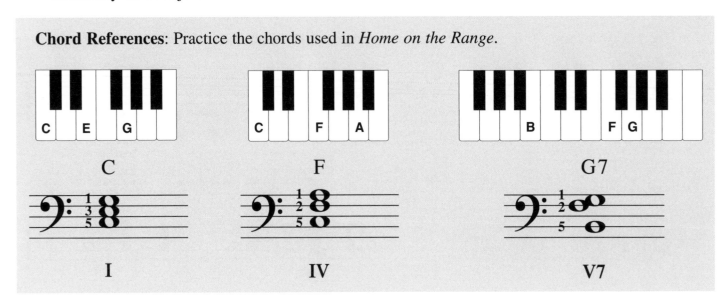

**Chord References**: Practice the chords used in *Home on the Range*.

**Directions:**

1. Play the melody only, with the damper pedal.
   (Note: Pedal marks are usually not included as part of a lead sheet.)

2. Then add L.H. **blocked chords** on *beat 1 of each measure* as indicated by the chord symbols.
   (If no chord symbol is present, repeat the chord of the previous measure.)

# Home on the Range

Traditional

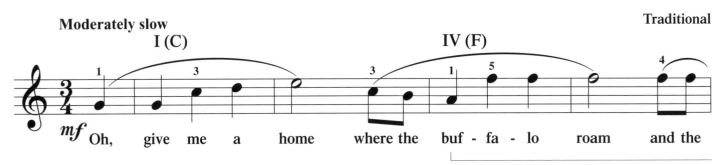

Moderately slow

*mf* Oh, give me a home where the buf - fa - lo roam and the

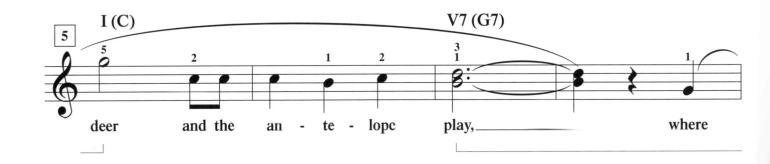

deer and the an - te - lopc play,_____ where

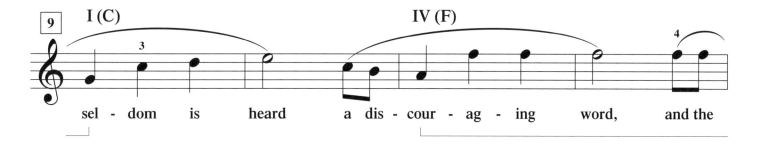

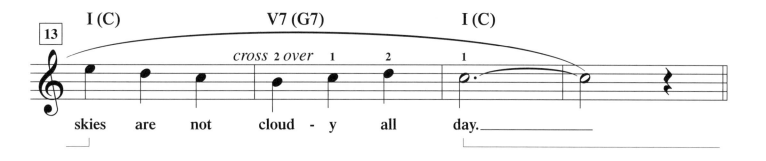

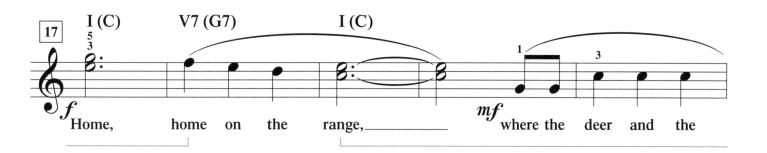

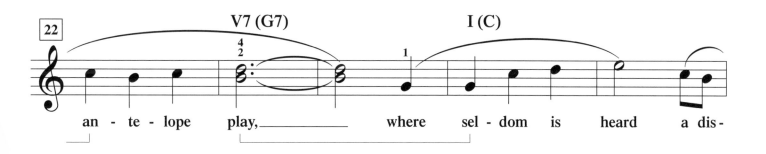

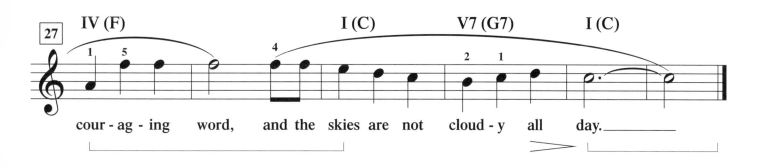

# The Damper Pedal

**Pedal markings**

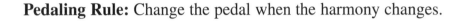

**Pedaling Rule:** Change the pedal when the harmony changes.

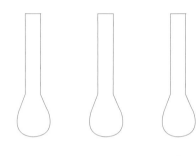

**1.** Trace the pedal marks for *mm. 1-2,* then continue writing your own pedal markings to the end.

- Identify the chords in *mm. 1-4* as **I**, **IV**, or **V7** in the boxes.

- Then harmonize *mm. 5-8* by writing **I**, **IV**, or **V7** chords on beats 2 and 3. Let your ears guide you.

## Pedaling the C Scale

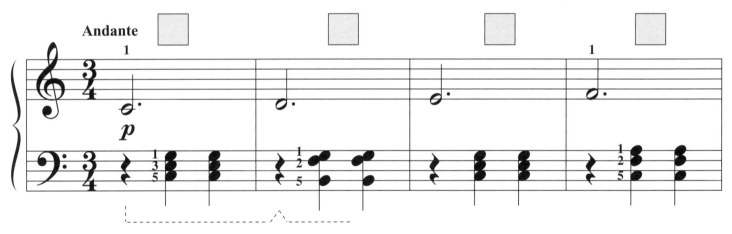

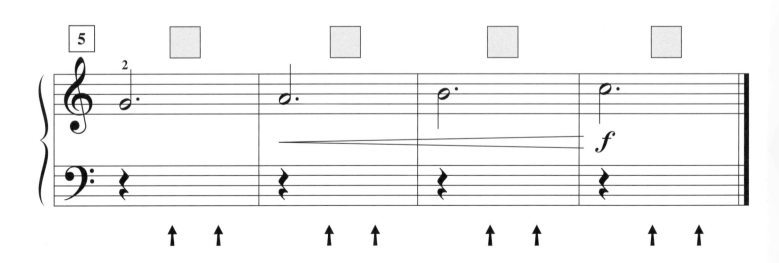

**2.** Play, with pedal. Can you come back down *harmonizing* the C scale?

FF

- First, scan the music and name each chord L.H. pattern as **I, IV, or V7**.

- Then sightread the examples below, without pedal.

- Play again using the pedal markings shown.

**Andante**

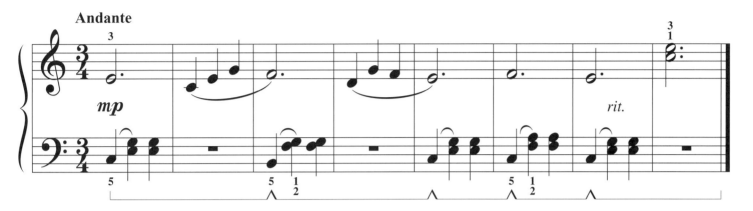

**Moderato**

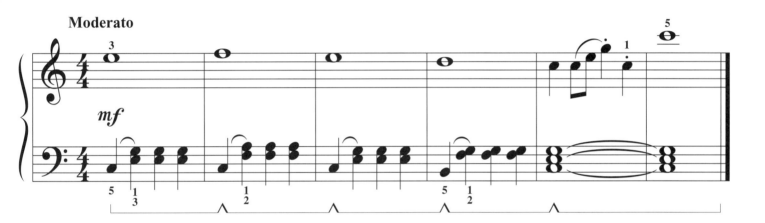

Write the Roman numerals, **I, IV,** or **V7** for each set of chords you hear.

For example, if your teacher says "Key of C" and plays this, you would write: **I  I  V7**.

1.

2.

3.

4.

# The Eighth Rest 𝄾

𝅘𝅥𝅮 + 𝅘𝅥𝅮 = 𝅘𝅥

½ + ½ = 1

𝄾 + 𝄾 = 𝄽

½ + ½ = 1

## Rock Band Rhythms

**1.** • Write **1 + 2 + 3 + 4 +** under the first measure for each example.

  • Name the **minor** pentascale used. Then play, counting aloud.

  • Try the "riff" hands together in low octaves.

——— pentascale

——— pentascale

——— pentascale

——— pentascale

**2. Improvisation with a Duet:**

  • Play the C minor accompaniment over and over while your teacher improvises using the **C minor pentascale**. Keep a great steady beat!

  • Then reverse. Let your teacher play the accompaniment while you improvise.

**C minor accompaniment**

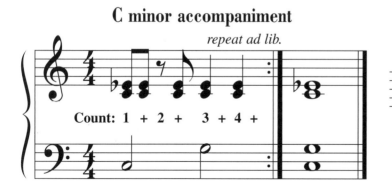

**C minor pentascale**

Improvise a melody using these notes in any order!

- Connect the boxes that have the *same* number of beats.

- Then write the **time signature** at the beginning of each.

Your teacher will play either example **a** or **b**. Circle the rhythm you hear.

(**Teacher Note:** Tap one "free" measure before playing. The examples may be played several times.)

**Extra Credit:** Now YOU be the teacher. Play either **a** or **b** of each example.
Let your teacher choose the answer.

Lessons p. 68

# The Dotted Quarter Note

The **dotted quarter note** usually is followed by a single **eighth note**.

1 + 2 + = 1 + 2 +

The tied eighth note is replaced by the **dot.**

• Tap and *feel* the tied eighth note. Then tap and *feel* the dot.

## Lead Sheet with ♩. ♪

**Directions:**

1. First tap and count *mm. 1-8. Feel* the dot on beat 2 for each ♩. ♪ rhythm.

2. Play the R.H. melody alone.

3. Play blocked L.H. chords while your teacher plays the melody.

4. Now add L.H. **blocked chords** on *beat 1* of each measure, as indicated by the chord symbols.

# Greensleeves

**Flowing smoothly**

English folk song

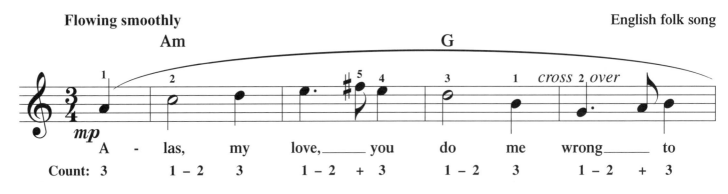

A - las, my love,_____ you do me wrong_____ to

Count: 3    1 – 2    3    1 – 2   +   3    1 – 2    3    1 – 2   +   3

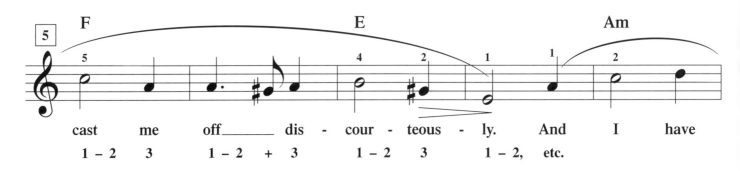

cast me off_____ dis - cour - teous - ly. And I have

1 – 2    3    1 – 2   +   3    1 – 2    3    1 – 2,   etc.

FF

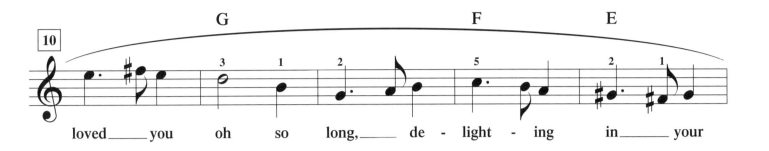

loved ___ you    oh    so    long, ___ de - light - ing    in ___ your

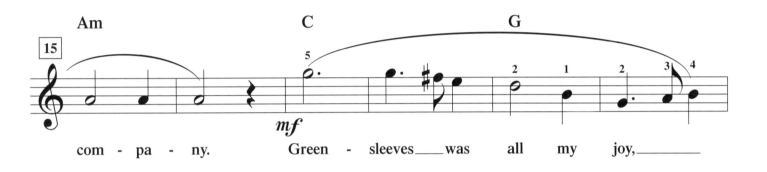

com - pa - ny.         Green - sleeves ___ was    all    my    joy, ___

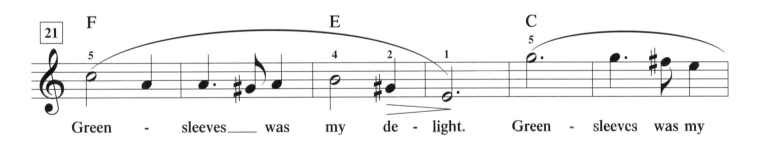

Green - sleeves ___ was    my    de - light.         Green - sleevcs    was    my

heart    of    gold, ___ and    who    but    my    la - dy    Green - sleeves.

# Composing with the Dotted Quarter Note

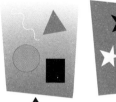  

A    B    A

This piece is in **ABA** form.
It has an **A section**, a **B section**, and return of the **A section**.

**Directions:**

**1.** Write the counts **1 + 2 + 3 +** (or simply **1   2 + 3**) for the opening **question** *(mm. 1-4)*.

  • Compose the **answer** *(mm. 5-8)*. Use the rhythm given above the staff.

  • Complete the L.H. melody for the **B** section *(mm. 9-16)*.
    Write the counts **1 + 2 + 3 +** below the music.

  • Play your dotted quarter note melody.

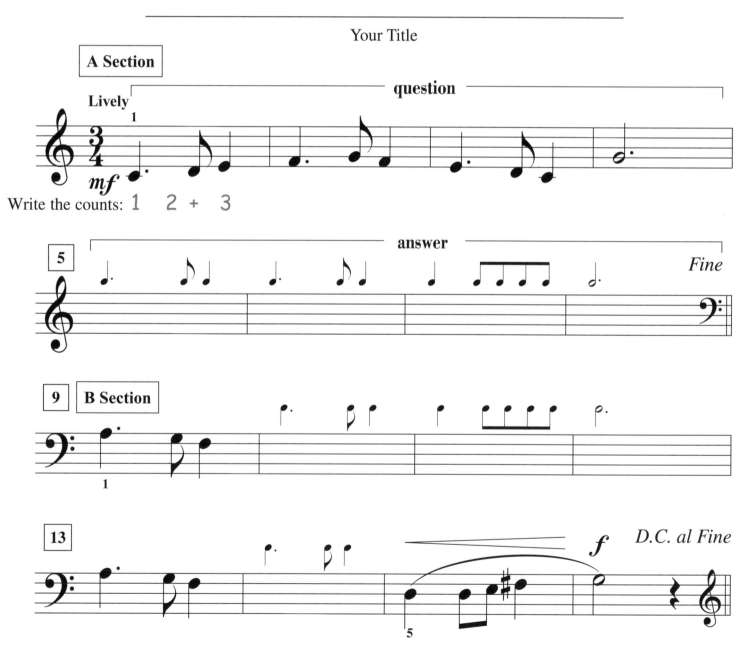

Your Title

**2. Super Student:** Write **I**, **IV**, or **V7** above each measure for the **A section**.
          Now play your **A B A** piece with L.H. blocked chords.

FF

- Before playing, circle each ♩. ♪ rhythm pattern.

- Sightread the music at a moderately slow tempo.

- Write a **I** or **V7** in the blank below each measure.
  Play again, with L.H. **blocked chords**.

**Moderato**

**Moderato**

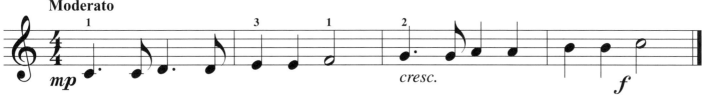

**Andante**

*(Right hand plays the chords)*

- First name the **major** or **minor pentascale** used for each example (Ex., D or Dm).
- Then your teacher will play rhythm **a** or **b**. Circle the rhythm you hear.

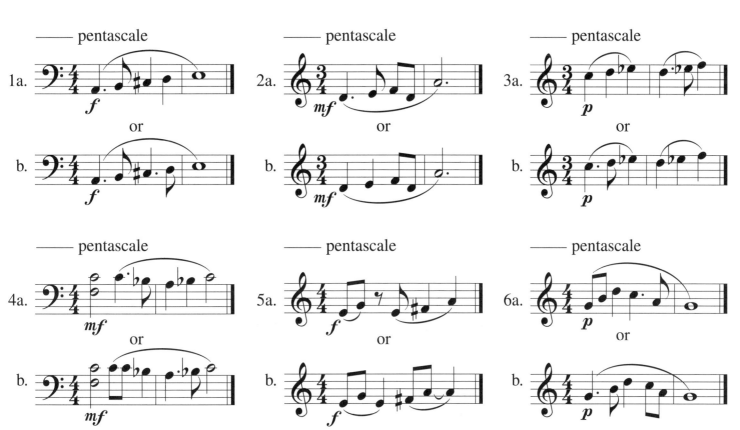

# The G Major Scale

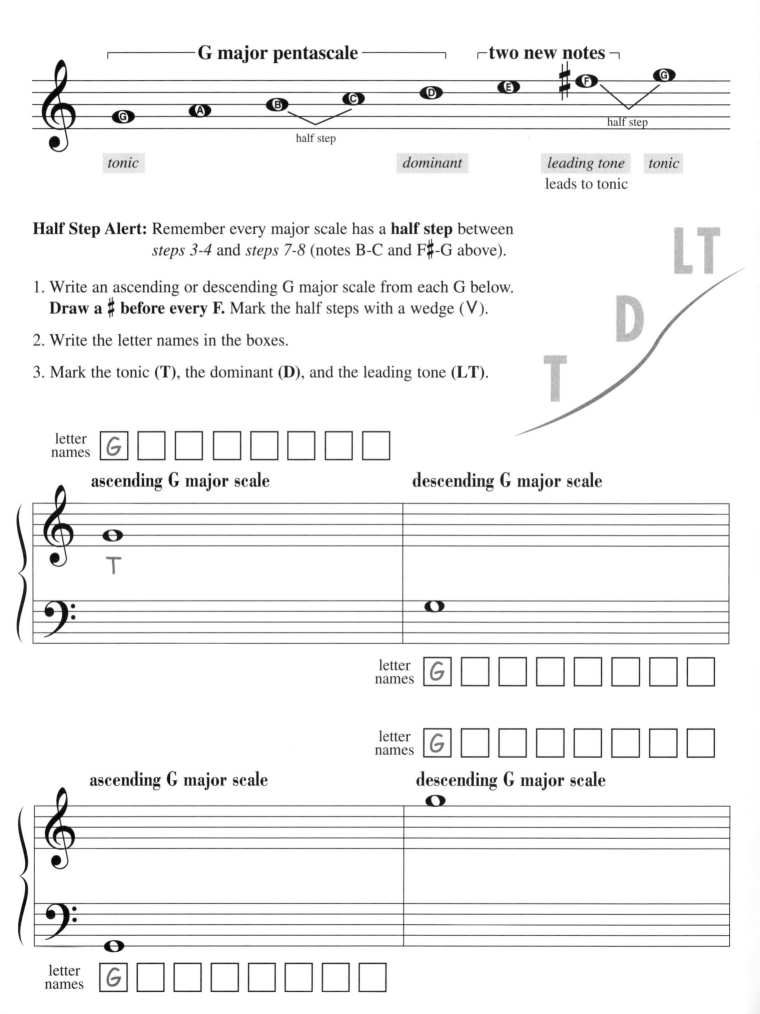

**Half Step Alert:** Remember every major scale has a **half step** between
*steps 3-4* and *steps 7-8* (notes B-C and F♯-G above).

1. Write an ascending or descending G major scale from each G below.
   **Draw a ♯ before every F.** Mark the half steps with a wedge (V).

2. Write the letter names in the boxes.

3. Mark the tonic (**T**), the dominant (**D**), and the leading tone (**LT**).

letter
names | G | | | | | | |

**ascending G major scale**  **descending G major scale**

letter
names | G | | | | | | |

letter
names | G | | | | | | |

**ascending G major scale**  **descending G major scale**

letter
names | G | | | | | | |

**Key signature for G Major:** Play all F's in the piece as **F-sharp**!

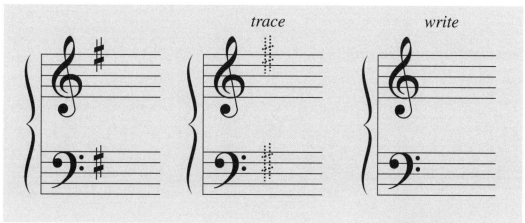

*trace*        *write*

- Answer the study questions below.

# Allegro

N. Faber

---

## A Closer Look at Allegro

### (Study Questions)

**1.** a. Write the key signature for G major (**F♯**) at the beginning of each line of music.

    b. Circle each **F♯** in the music.

    c. The form of this piece is **A B**. Label each section in your music.

    d. Label the two **questions** and **answers**. Write *parallel* or *contrasting* for each answer.

**2.** Now play *Allegro*. If a digital keyboard is available, play using the harpsichord or string setting.

Lessons p.78

# Lead Sheet in G Major

**Chord References:** Practice the chords used in *For He's a Jolly Good Fellow*.

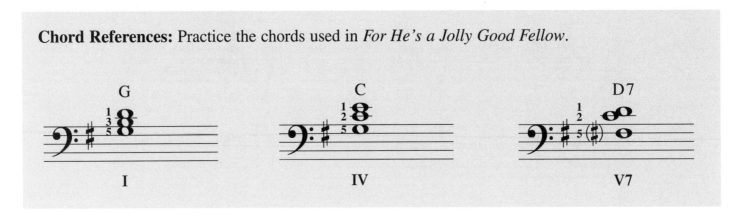

**Directions:**

1. First, play the melody only.

2. Then add L.H. **blocked chords** on *beat 1 of each measure* as indicated by the chord symbols.

# For He's a Jolly Good Fellow

Traditional

For he's a jol - ly good fel - low, for

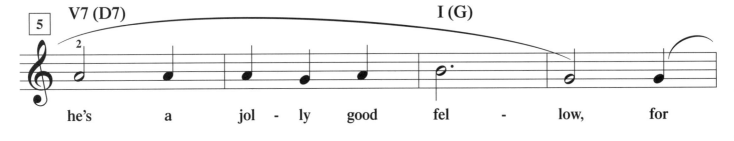

he's a jol - ly good fel - low, for

he's a jol - ly good fel - low, that

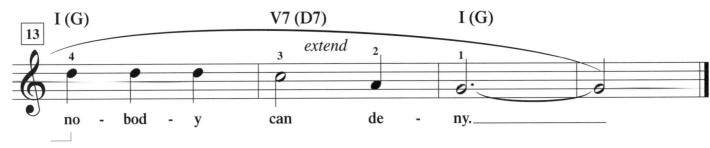

no - bod - y can de - ny.

- Clap *measure 1* for your teacher.
  Put a ✔ above each measure with this pattern: ♪♪ 𝄾 ♪ ♪♪

- Sightread the melody. Then **harmonize** the melody by writing
  **I**, **IV**, or **V7** in the boxes. Play again, using L.H. blocked chords.

**Improvisation with the G Major Scale**

FEEL THE BEAT!

- Your teacher (or a friend) will play the duet below.
  First, *listen* and feel the beat.

*R.H.*  **G major scale**

- When you are ready, improvise a melody using
  notes from the **G major scale** in any order.
  Use *2nds* and *3rds*. Begin and end on **G** (the tonic).

**Duet:** (Student improvises *higher* on the keyboard.)

*Repeat over and over* | **Ending**

Lessons p. 84

# The F Major Scale

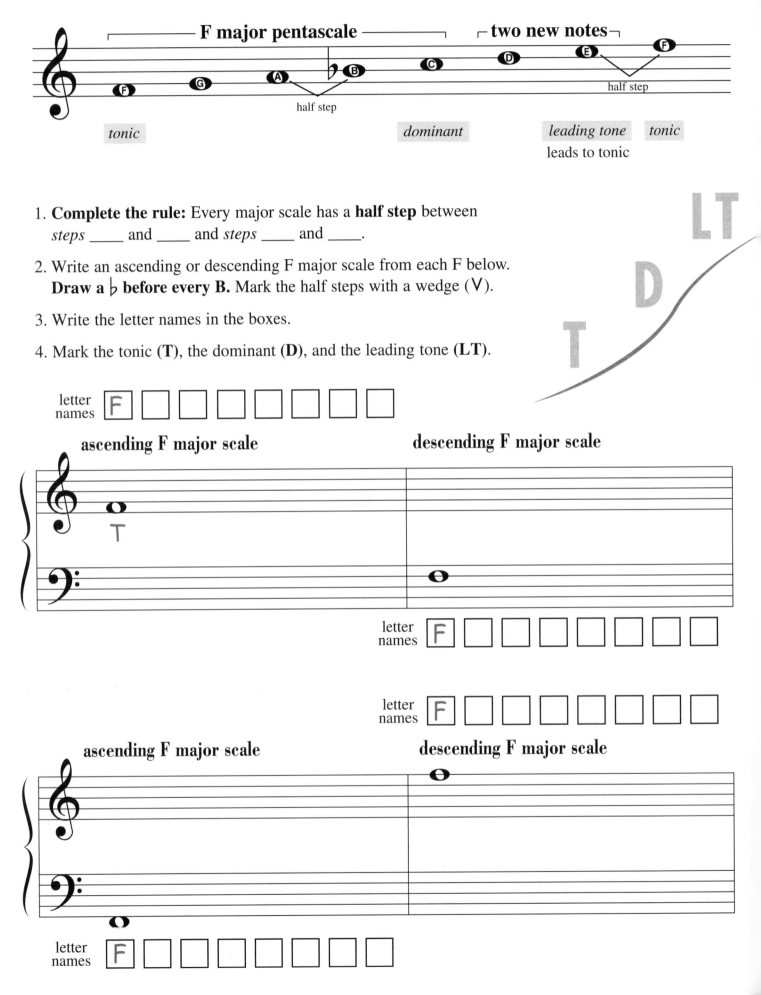

1. **Complete the rule:** Every major scale has a **half step** between
   *steps* _____ and _____ and *steps* _____ and _____.

2. Write an ascending or descending F major scale from each F below.
   **Draw a ♭ before every B.** Mark the half steps with a wedge (∨).

3. Write the letter names in the boxes.

4. Mark the tonic (**T**), the dominant (**D**), and the leading tone (**LT**).

**Key signature for F Major:** Play all B's in the piece as **B-flat**!

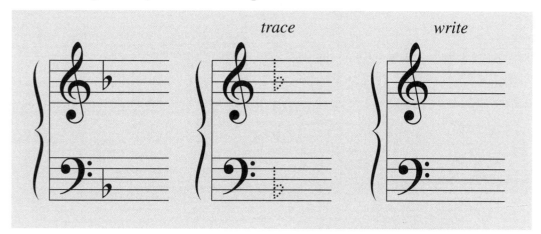

*trace*          *write*

**1.** • Complete this lullaby by composing a *parallel* or *contrasting* answer for each question.

• Circle all the **B-flats**.

• Play your *ABA Lullaby*.

# ABA Lullaby

question

answer

*Fine*

5

9

5

13

*D.C. al Fine*

**2. Super Student:** • Label the **form.**

• Add your own slurs to show musical ideas.

# Lead Sheet in F Major

**Chord References:** Practice the chords used in *The Londonderry Air*.

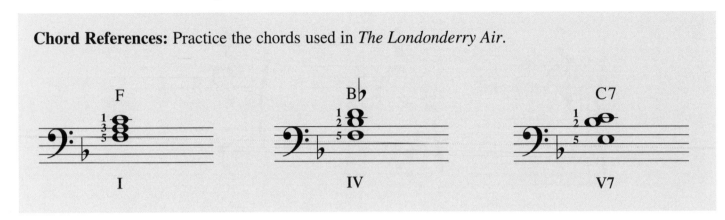

## Directions:

1. First, play the melody alone carefully observing the fingering.

2. Then add L.H. **blocked chords** on *beat 1 of each measure* as indicated by the chord symbols.

# The Londonderry Air

Notice there is no chord on the opening *upbeats*.

**English folk song**

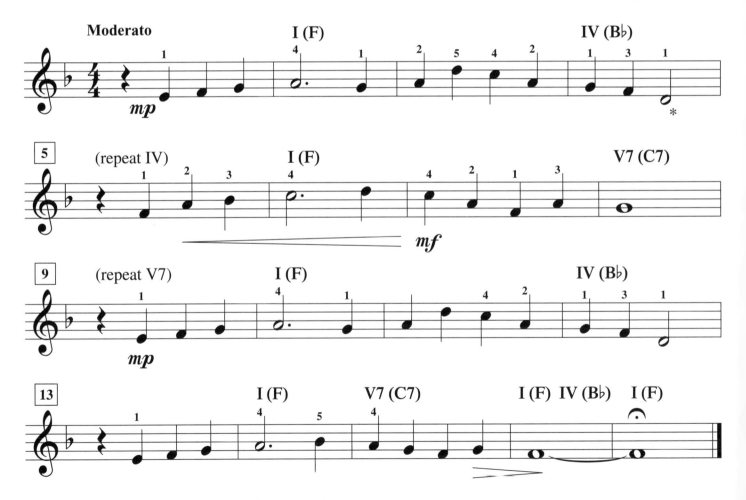

*Release the L.H. thumb (of the B♭ chord) for the melody note D.

- Write the Roman numerals below the staff (**I, IV, V7**).

- Sightread while your teacher plays the duet.

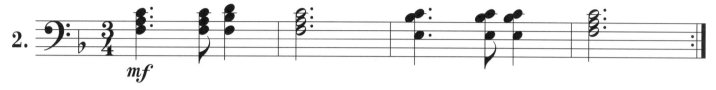

**Teacher Duets**

# Improvisation with the F Major Scale

- Your teacher (or a friend) will play the duet below. First, *listen* and feel the beat.

- When you are ready, improvise a melody using notes from the **F major scale** in any order. Use *2nds* and *3rds*. Begin and end on F (the tonic).

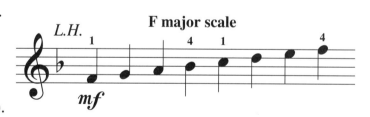

**Duet:** (Student improvises *higher* on the keyboard)

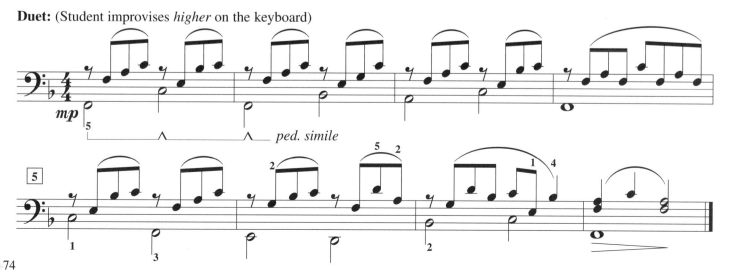

74

# Final Review

- Complete this crossword puzzle and review 18 musical terms!

- The answers are given upside down at the bottom of the page.

# Musical Terms Crossword Puzzle

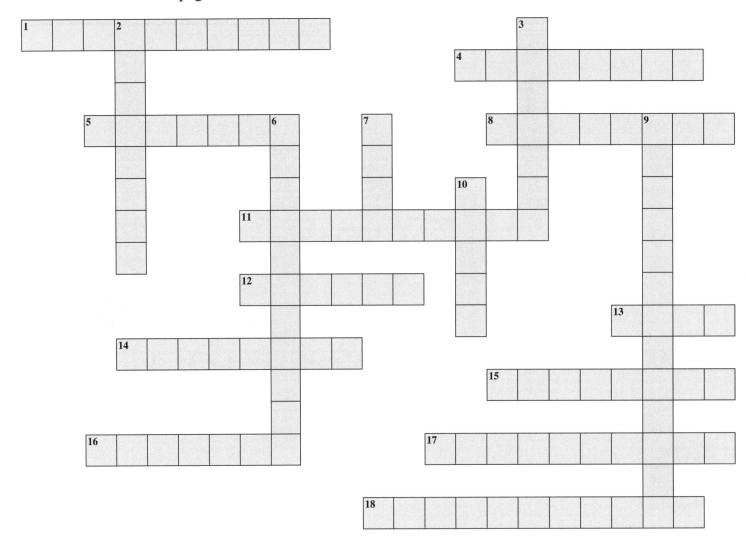

## Across

1. A gradual slowing down of the tempo.
4. Notes moving in opposite directions.
5. Hold this note longer than usual.
8. The distance from one key to the very closest key.
11. Five-note scale.
12. A short line used to extend the staff.
13. The musical plan of a piece.
14. The fifth step of the scale.
15. The "louds and softs" of music.
16. Fast. Lively tempo.
17. Very soft.
18. The seventh step of the scale.

## Down

2. "Harp-like." The notes of a chord played one after another.
3. Walking tempo.
6. Play gradually faster.
7. Ending section.
9. Playing music in a differrent key.
10. Whole-whole-half-whole pattern.

*Across:* 1. ritardando 4. contrary 5. fermata 8. half step 11. pentascale 12. ledger 13. form 14. dominant 15. dynamics 16. allegro 17. pianissimo 18. leading tone

*Down:* 2. arpeggio 3. andante 6. accelerando 7. coda 9. transposition 10. major

64

FF